Louis Riel Rosemary Neering

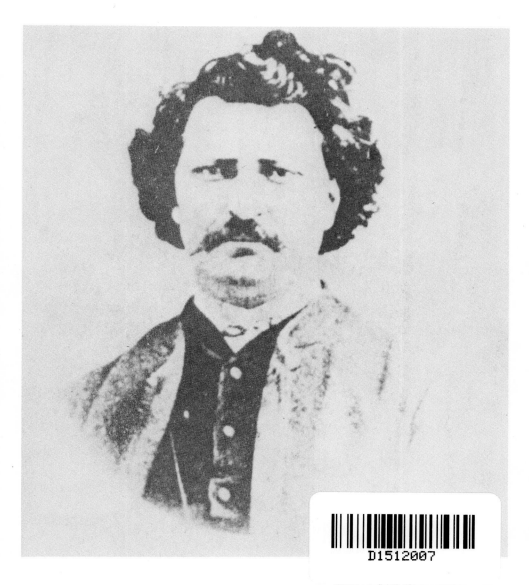

D1512007

Fitzhenry & Whiteside Limited

Contents

The Author

Rosemary Neering lives in Victoria, B.C., and is the author of several titles dealing with the history of the Canadian West.

© 1977 Fitzhenry & Whiteside Limited
150 Lesmill Road
Don Mills, Ontario M3B 2T5

Printed and bound in Canada

ISBN-0-88902-214-3

The Buffalo Hunt Chapter 1

The wooden wheels of the Red River carts screeched in
protest and the dust rose high in the air as the train of
carts groaned slowly westward across the plains. West
from the spring meeting place at Pembina went the Métis,
west from Red River, west in search of the buffalo that
roamed and grazed the wide prairie country.

Every eye was keen on the distance. The success of
the buffalo hunt would decide everything for the year to
come. If the Métis had a good hunt, they would have food
to eat and pemmican to trade for supplies. If they found
no buffalo, the year would be difficult.

This year of 1840, the cart train stretched out almost
ten kilometres, more than 1,200 carts long. The guide's
flag flew, strong and steady, at the front as he led the
buffalo hunters westward.

At six o'clock, the Métis made camp. Captains and
soldiers in the Métis organization hastened each cart into
place in the camp and fires were lit. On a small hill outside
the huge ring of carts, the guides and leaders met to talk
and smoke in the gathering dusk.

*A Métis brigade setting out
to hunt buffalo*

Early the next morning, the train was underway again. No buffalo were yet in sight. The next day followed as the first and the second: only the flat land stretching away to the horizon with the dry grass parched under the sun. Once, far in the distance, a rider bent for some unknown destination showed against the sky. Once a group of Indians appeared briefly and was gone.

For nineteen days, the trek continued without a glimpse of the great shaggy animals that the Métis sought. Food grew scarce; there was no game.

Then on the twentieth day, there they were — the ponderous, brown, bearded animals far out ahead. The guide dropped his flag. Excitement caught hold of the Métis. Quickly, the captains shuffled everyone into a makeshift camp. Four hundred hunters brought their nervous, pawing horses into line.

Then, "Start!" the hunt captain yelled, and the chase began. At first, the hunters trotted their horses slowly toward the buffalo. Then they broke into a furious gallop. They were perhaps five hundred metres away when the buffalo sensed there were enemies nearby.

The bulls' tails curved up. A thousand feet pawed the ground. Then they were off, fleeing, dust grinding up

"Métis running the buffalo" from the painting by Paul Kane

over their heads. But it was too late. The hunters were at full speed and already their trained horses were among the buffalo.

Zigzagging through the herd they went, the hunters firing from a metre or two away, rifles gripped in one hand, shot clenched in the mouth for reloading, knees guiding the horses, hugging them, directing them as they twisted this way and that among the huge beasts, the fat cows falling to the dust, noise like thunder with the hooves of buffalo and horse echoing along the open prairie.

Then it was over. Almost a thousand buffalo lay dead, their carcasses dumped heavily to the ground. The rest of the herd had outdistanced the hunters, terror lending them speed. The hunters turned their horses back towards the kill.

Each hunter knew at a glance which beasts he had killed. As he drew his sharp knife to begin skinning and butchering each animal, the carts pulled up behind and the women loaded the meat. Tomorrow, the slow process of drying the meat in the sun and making pemmican would begin.

Back in camp, the air was joyous. It had been a good

A Métis home

hunt and the Métis knew the year to come would be equally good. For them, the buffalo hunts were the high points of the year, the times when the group came so closely together that all thought and acted as one.

These hunts were what kept them from being merely farmers or storekeepers. And mere farmers or store-keepers they would never be. The Métis were the descendants of their Indian mothers whose tribes had freely roamed the West, who had lived on the land and were the rulers of it. They were also descended from their fur trader fathers who had come to the plains with the Hudson's Bay or the North West Company to open trading posts and trade or trap for furs. This combination, the Métis knew, made them something special, a race apart, a people who had the right to live as they wished, free, strong, and lords of their country.

Most of them lived near the Red River, grouped into settlements of French, English and Scottish Métis. From there, they drove the Red River carts that carried goods north and south between the Hudson's Bay Company community at Red River and the American settlements to the south. They hunted the buffalo and traded the pemmican to the fur traders in exchange for supplies, and they acted as intermediaries between the traders and the Indians. They had developed a society all their own.

1849: Chapter 2
The Trial of Guillaume Sayer

The crowd of men surged along the east bank of the Red
River, shouting and arguing among themselves. Some
waved their rifles and buffalo guns as they talked, gestur-
ing angrily toward the walls of Fort Garry on the far side
of the river. Then the boats and canoes arrived, gathered
from every corner of the French Métis community at
Red River.

   The men swarmed into the boats and across the river.
Up the bank they went, through the wide gates of the fort
and along the dusty street to the wooden courthouse.
There they milled about in front of the closed door, firing
their guns into the air. One voice sounded above the
others.

*Fort Garry, the seat of Riel's
government*

"They have arrested one of us, a Métis, and for what? Because he dared to buy and sell furs when the great and mighty Hudson's Bay Company said he could not! And why do they say that? Because they want everything for themselves. They want to make all the rules and let no one else speak — especially if they speak in French!"

The man who harangued the crowd was the same man who had urged them, the Sunday before, to make this trip across the river. His name was Louis Riel. Once, in Quebec, he had wanted to be a priest, but the excitement of the North-West had called him back. Now he was a miller on the banks of the river; more important, he was one of the most vocal of the Métis leaders.

"Will we stand for this?" Riel demanded. "Will we stand meekly here and let someone else tell us what to do, someone who does not care what we want? We say that trade shall be free, and we shall buy and sell whenever and from whomever we want!"

A great cheer sounded off the walls of the fort. Suddenly, the cheer changed to angry shouts. The judge and his retinue had slipped in through a back door of the courthouse, and now the court clerk was calling the name of Guillaume Sayer, a Métis accused of dealing illegally in furs.

The Métis waiting outside demanded that Sayer be tried by a jury of his own choosing and that he be allowed to take some of his fellow Métis into the courtroom with him. The judge, aware of the men waiting at the courthouse door, agreed. Twelve Métis entered the courtroom; twenty more stood guard at the door; another fifty waited at the outer door. The rest remained outside.

Inside the courtroom, Judge Adam Thom tugged the neckband of his robe away from his sweating skin. By the laws of the land and the Hudson's Bay Company, Sayer was guilty as charged. Even the jury chosen by Sayer himself had now found him guilty. But would it be wise — or even possible, with the armed men standing in the courthouse — to punish Sayer? Thom swallowed nervously and made up his mind.

"Guillaume Sayer, you have been found guilty as charged," he began, and a low growl spread outward from the Métis grouped near the door, "but . . . but . . ." Thom held up a hand, "I shall let you go free."

Louis Riel, Senior (right). The man on the left is thought to be Guillaume Sayer.

The Métis cheered wildly. Outside, the guns were fired in joy and the crowd chanted: "La commerce est libre; vive la liberté!" Shouting and jostling, the men carried Sayer back toward the river and the Métis community of St. Boniface.

That night, Sayer's release was the topic of conversation in every home in St. Boniface. "It is just the beginning," Louis Riel said to his wife. "We have shown the Hudson's Bay Company that they cannot stamp on us. The Métis will not stand for tyranny. We are a nation and we have the right to make our own laws."

The eyes of the Riels' five-year-old son Louis glowed as he listened to words he barely understood. "Papa," he shouted, "Papa, I will help, I will help fight."

Louis Riel père swung the small boy up onto his shoulder. "You, my son? You have a long way to go yet. All you could do now would be to bite the enemy on the knee. But you have spirit and perhaps one day you will be a leader."

"If God wills it," said Julie Riel softly. "You must always work in the service of God, my son."

Louis fils barely heard his mother's words. He was lost in a dream that saw him riding a great horse, leading men in battle, winning, always winning.

Julie Lagimodiere Riel

Chapter 3 **Growing Up**

Louis Riel's hands trembled as he took the wafer from the hands of the priest and touched his lips to the cup of wine. The sounds around him in the cathedral at St. Boniface slipped away and he was alone with his love for God. Ever since he was a small child, he had been waiting for this day, for his First Communion in the Catholic Church. He prayed silently that he would be worthy of God's love.

In the pews behind him, Louis' mother watched her son with proud eyes. Once she had desired with all her soul to be a nun, but her parents had decided she was to marry instead. Now she prayed her eldest son might serve God as she had once longed to do.

The young Louis Riel had grown up on the east side of the Red River near St. Boniface. There he saw the

St. Boniface Cathedral

buffalo hunts, the yearly trips to the lake shore to shoot geese and the cart trains that lumbered across the prairie; he heard the rousing music of the Métis dances that lasted all night and the flaming rhetoric of his father's political speeches.

Yet the young boy was most affected by his life at home and at school. The Riel family was very religious and its members very close to one another. Louis learned his first lessons at home, then went in turn to the small schools taught by the Grey Sisters, a group of nuns, and the Christian Brothers, a group of priests.

By the time he was thirteen and ready for his First Communion, Louis had reached the end of any schooling he could find in Red River. Monseigneur Taché, the Bishop of Red River, had watched the school careers of Louis and other young Métis boys with interest; he was determined that some of them should be educated further so that they could return to Red River and help their

Bishop Alexandre A. Taché

Louis Riel, 1858

people. He chose Louis and three other boys to go to school in Quebec, where they would study at Catholic colleges.

The parents of one of the boys would not let him go. The others — Riel, Daniel McDougall and Louis Schmidt — set off for the East one spring day in 1858. Once more the wheels of the Red River carts screeched as the Métis tripmen headed south. This time, they carried the three boys with them.

Every turn of the wheel took Louis further away from home. As he waved goodbye, especially to his mother and his young sister Sarah, he felt a wrench inside him at the thought of leaving behind this familiar place to live in a big and bustling city with people he did not know. For a moment he was not at all sure that he wanted to go. He wished he could talk to his father about the trip, but the elder Riel was somewhere between Montreal and Red River, on his way home after buying new machinery for a mill.

The cart train moved on leaving Fort Garry behind. It went slowly south, making barely 30 kilometres a day. At last it reached the ferry that would take the boys across the Mississippi. There, disembarking, was a familiar figure.

A Red River ox cart

"Papa," Louis shouted, dropping from the cart and racing across the ground toward his father.

The two shook hands gravely. There was very little time to talk before Louis must take the ferry. "Montreal is such a very long way away," stuttered Louis, "and I shall miss you all very much. Are you sure that I should go?"

"Yes, my son. The Métis will need educated men to lead them in the times ahead when all the world is changing. If you become a priest, then you will serve both God and your people. Go, study hard, learn to serve God with all your heart. Then you can return to Red River."

Louis looked up at his father for a minute, then suddenly hugged him hard and raced off toward the ferry.

From St. Paul, the three boys travelled by train. There was so much new to see: the steaming trains themselves, so swift and so complex compared to the Red River carts; the teeming crowds in the American cities they passed through; the fashionably dressed men and women who climbed aboard the train. Then came Montreal itself, with no sign of the rough and friendly people Louis was used to at home. But he was no longer afraid. His father had told him to come to Montreal; he would make his father and his family proud.

Chapter 4 **End of the Dream**

Louis Riel paced up and down his small room at the college, four steps one way, three the other, forward and back, forward and back. Then he stood staring out the window at the snow that covered the ground in the courtyard. His seventh year in Montreal and his world had fallen apart.

He remembered so well the trip from Red River to Montreal six years before, his last meeting with his father, the dreams his father had for him. Now the news had reached Montreal: his father was dead: "Why?" Louis whispered to the cold, empty room. "Why did he have to die? Why couldn't I have seen him just once more? I would have made him so proud."

He turned away from the window, back to the desk that was littered with crumpled scraps of paper, where he had tried and failed to write some words of comfort to his family, his responsibility now. "My dear Papa always gave us such an example," he wrote. "Papa, dear Papa, you will care for us still in Heaven above. We will pray for you. Let us have courage and faith in God."

It was impossible for Louis to follow his own advice. For the past six years he had studied at the College of Montreal. His work had been good; often he had ranked in the top five in his class. Now, with the death of his father, it all seemed pointless. He could not bring himself to obey the restrictive rules at the college; he wanted to escape and take responsibility for his own life. The priests were too strict with him and the old classrooms too cramped and airless and oppressive. Perhaps he was not meant to be a priest. Perhaps God had other plans for him.

For almost a year after the death of his father, Riel struggled with his deepening desire to abandon his studies. Then he made up his mind. All around him the people of Quebec were questioning this new union with Ontario that would make the two colonies one country. Could the French keep their language, their heritage and their religion? Or would they be swept away in a torrent of English-speaking people who would outnumber the

This early 19th century drawing gives an impression of a lawyer's office. Conditions would probably not have changed much by the time Riel became a lawyer's clerk.

French? These were the same questions the Métis asked in the West, and Riel felt a strong kinship with the French and a fierce desire to learn more about the situation.

He left the college and plunged into a world alive with debate and political argument. His long training in logic and politics made him able to debate with almost anyone and he immediately felt at home. He took a job as a clerk in a law office, hoping that he might perhaps eventually become a lawyer or a politician. Every evening he met with the other young men of Montreal, to argue and question and debate.

Far below the slopes of the mountain that overlooks Montreal, the waters of the St. Lawrence glinted blue and the ships moved to and fro in the harbour. But Louis Riel looked only at the girl who lay beside him on the grass. He took her hand in his, then pulled her closer to him.

"Marie, marry me. I am nothing now, but one day I will be famous and able to provide well for you."

Marie Guernon pulled away and shook her head. "Louis, don't be silly. You know I can't marry you. My parents would be furious if they suspected I was here with you. You know they don't like you; they would never let me be your wife."

"What does that matter? All your father can do is yell and shout, as usual. If you loved me, you'd marry me."

"I do love you. But I can't . . ."

"Yes, you can. No one can stop us. Come on."

He pulled Marie to her feet and ran with her down toward the city.

A betrothal contract was drawn up and the banns announcing that Louis Riel and Marie Guernon were to be married were posted in the Church of the Holy Infant Jesus. Scarcely had they appeared when Joseph Guernon came storming down the street to the house where Louis Riel stayed with his aunt and uncle.

"You — you — you think you can marry my daughter," he spluttered, his face purple with anger. "You, a Métis, a savage, a man without a job, without a penny, a man who ran away from school. You have nothing. You are nothing. I have sent Marie away and you will not see her again." Guernon stormed out of the house, slamming the door behind him.

Riel stared at the closed door, his mind spinning. So this was what these French really thought of him. Not good enough for a French girl, not good enough for Montreal people.

He made a sudden decision. If this was what Montreal thought of him, he would leave Montreal. He had been away from home too long; it was time to go back to Red River.

Return to Red River
Chapter 5

The voice of Louis Riel rang out over the crowd that had gathered in front of St. Boniface Cathedral. "These men have come from Canada to take our land away from us. What right have they to touch one grain of our soil? What right have they to measure, to survey, to steal what is ours? We did not ask the Hudson's Bay Company to sell us to Canada — they did not own us! We will not let these Canadians push us around!"

The Louis Riel who spoke was far different from the uncertain thirteen-year-old who had left Red River eleven years before. This was a tall, handsome man, with compelling eyes that caught and held the listener fast. His voice was strong and sure. Every word he spoke showed the years he had spent studying in Montreal and

Riel and his council, 1870

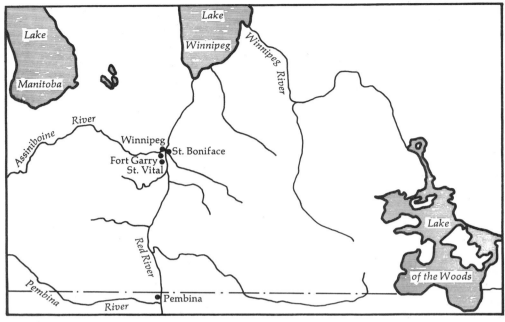

RED RIVER AREA

the things he had learned there. The assurance in his manner and his voice reflected the hundreds of evenings he had spent in debate in Montreal and the experience gained from his travels through the United States on his way home to Red River.

Red River had changed as well. Fort Garry was now flanked by the growing town of Winnipeg and settlers had hurried west from Canada to take up land there. Most important, the Hudson's Bay Company had agreed to sell its territory in the North-West to Canada; it remained only for the transfer to take place.

In preparation for this transfer, the Canadian government had sent a surveying party to Red River. The survey would divide the land into square sections, each two square kilometres in size and shape, ready for settlers to claim when they arrived. But, as was traditional also in Quebec, the Métis had long ago laid out their farms in long narrow strips facing the river, with every farmer having some river frontage, some of the good land near the water, and a haying privilege on the land behind that. The Métis feared this new Canadian survey would cut across these long-established farms.

Winnipeg, 1869. The flag, which has the word "Canada" on it, marks Dr. Schultz's drugstore.

Fort Garry. Who built the fort?

The survey seemed just one sign of the way things were to be. Although arrangements were well under way for Canada to take over the North-West, no one had consulted the people there about what they wanted. Instead, it seemed, all the arrangements were to be made in Ottawa.

One group in the settlement seemed well pleased with these arrangements. These were the "Canadians", people who had come west in the last few years in anticipation of Canada's taking over the area. They were openly contemptuous of the Métis, referring to them as dirty, lazy and worthless. The sooner Canada took over and threw the Métis out, the happier these people would be.

It was not long before the bad feeling on both sides

A settler with his effects in Saskatchewan

erupted into a quarrel. The Métis were at a meeting discussing the problems when André Nault, a cousin of Riel, burst into the room.

"The surveyors are running a line across my haying land," he shouted.

The Métis raced from the building and swung onto their horses. In minutes, they had galloped to Nault's land. There, eighteen men, unarmed, stood in a grim line over the surveyor's chain.

"What do you think you're doing?" demanded one of the surveyors.

"You are trespassing on this land. We will move from this chain only if you promise to stop your survey and leave. Go back to Canada and tell the government there that this is not their country yet and we will not stand silent while Canadians steal our land."

The surveyors looked at each other, then at the crowd of Métis. It seemed wisest to leave Nault's land.

Not all the battles would be that simple. That same month — October 1869 — the Métis learned that the Canadian government was sending William McDougall to take over as lieutenant-governor of the North-West — even though the transfer of the land to Canada had not yet taken place.

Hastily, a National Committee of the Métis was formed to decide what to do about McDougall. Shortly afterwards, Métis messengers rode south to intercept the new governor.

They located him just as he crossed the border from the United States. Silently, they handed him a written message: "The National Committee of the Métis of Red River orders William McDougall not to enter the territory of the North-West without special permission of the above-mentioned committee."

McDougall squinted through the sunshine at the men on horseback. "And who do you think you are to stop a representative of the Queen and the Canadian government? Move aside. I will pass."

He rode on to the first Hudson's Bay post across the border. There, a second Métis patrol intercepted him.

"You will leave this territory at once," commanded Ambrose Lépine, leader of the patrol.

"By whose authority?"

"By the authority of the people of Red River whom I represent."

"I do not accept any such authority."

Lépine cocked his revolver and held it steady, trained on McDougall. "Canada has no rights in this country yet, and by the same token, neither have you. We have come to see that you return to the United States immediately — in whatever condition you prefer. Go now, or accept the consequences."

McDougall stared at Lépine and at the revolver. He knew he had no legal right to enter the North-West as its governor until Canada formally took possession of the area. Perhaps he would be wiser to wait. He glared at the Métis a moment longer, then turned his own horse south, back toward the border.

Chapter 6 **Provisional Government**

Red River was in turmoil as soon as the news spread that McDougall had been turned back at the border. The Hudson's Bay Council that governed the North-West summoned Riel to a meeting to account for the Métis actions. Riel told them that the Métis had no objection to HBC rule, but that they would not stand idly by while a new government imposed its will on the North-West. If Canada wished to take over the area, then it must send representatives to discuss the transfer and the future status of Red River.

The explanation did not satisfy everyone. The Canadians around Fort Garry were outraged that such treatment had been meted out to a representative of Canada. Led by Dr. John Schultz and Major Charles Boulton, they began to talk loudly about how they would stop the Métis from any similar actions.

The Métis heard about the Canadian meetings and feared that the Canadians would try to take over Fort Garry from the Hudson's Bay Company and establish their own control over the Red River settlement. They decided to act first.

Early one morning, they crossed the river in twos and threes until more than 100 Métis had slipped into the fort through the governor's private entrance. Quietly, they took over the fort; since they formed the only armed group in the settlement no one could challenge their possession.

Métis patrols fanned out along the roads leading to the fort to make sure no trouble occurred. At the fort, Riel called a meeting to try to explain why he and his men had acted as they had.

By taking the initiative Riel and the other Métis split the community. Some said that they were now rebels against the Crown. Riel angrily denied this. "If we are rebels," he cried, "we are rebels against the company that

sold us and is ready to hand us over, and against Canada
that wants to buy us. We do not rebel against Britain.
We are protecting our native land against the dangers
that threaten us. We want the people of Red River to be
a free people. Let us help one another. Let us unite."

Two days later, representatives from all parts of
Red River came to the fort to take part in a convention
that would determine what should happen next. Riel
wanted to form a provisional government, with the power
to represent the area in any dealings with the Canadian
government. For days, the Métis and the other settlers
argued over whether this would be rebellion. Finally,
Riel lost patience.

"Go, return peacefully to your farms," he boomed
out. "Stay in the arms of your wives. Give this example
to your children. But watch us act. We are going ahead
to work to obtain the guarantee of our rights and yours.
You will come to share them in the end."

The community finally agreed on one thing: they
would put together a bill of rights for Red River. The bill
demanded an elected legislature, representation in the
Canadian parliament and recognition of both English
and French as official languages in the area. Preparations
were made to take the bill of rights to Ottawa and present
it to the government.

*Sir John A. Macdonald,
about 1872*

Riel and his men were still worried that the Canadians
would try to overrun Fort Garry and destroy what the
Métis had accomplished. To forestall them, the Métis
marched to Dr. Shultz's store and arrested him and 47
other Canadians; they were imprisoned in Fort Garry.

At last, the Canadian government awoke to the fact
that something was wrong in the West. The prime
minister, John A. Macdonald, and his main Quebec
lieutenant, George Cartier, decided to send Donald Smith,
head of the Hudson's Bay Company in Canada, to determine what grievances the Red River settlers had, and to
explain to the settlers what the Canadian government
planned to do.

Riel was suspicious, but he agreed to talk to Smith.
Despite his fears, he was impressed by this reasonable,
calm man. He agreed to act as interpreter for Smith so
that he could explain the situation to the Métis. In —30° C
weather, Smith and Riel spoke on for hours to the large

LIST OF RIGHTS.

1. That the people have the right to elect their own Legislature.

2. That the Legislature have the power to pass all laws local to the Territory over the veto of the Executive by a two-thirds vote.

3. That no act of the Dominion Parliament (local to the Territory) be binding on the people until sanctioned by the Legislature of the Territory.

4. That all Sheriffs, Magistrates, Constables, School Commissioners, etc., be elected by the people.

5. A free Homestead and pre-emption Land Law.

6. That a portion of the public lands be appropriated to the benefit of Schools, the building of Bridges, Roads and Public Buildings.

7. That it be guaranteed to connect Winnipeg by Rail with the nearest line of Railroad, within a term of five years ; the land grant to be subject to the Local Legislature.

8. That for the term of four years all Military, Civil, and Municipal expenses be paid out of the Dominion funds.

9. That the Military be composed of the inhabitants now existing in the Territory.

10. That the English and French languages be common in the Legislature and Courts, and that all Public Documents and Acts of the Legislature be published in both languages.

11. That the Judge of the Supreme Court speak the English and French languages.

12. That Treaties be concluded and ratified between the Dominion Government and the several tribes of Indians in the Territory to ensure peace on the frontier.

13. That we have a fair and full representation in the Canadian Parliament.

14. That all privileges, customs and usages existing at the time of the transfer be respected.

All the above articles have been severally discussed and adopted by the French and Eeglish Representatives without a dissenting voice, as the conditions upon which the people of Rupert's Land enter into Confederation.

The French Representatives then proposed in order to secure the above rights, that a Delegation be appointed and sent to Pembina to see Mr. Macdougall and ask him if he could guarantee these rights by virtue of his commission ; and if he could do so, that then the French people would join to a man to escort Mr. Macdougall into his Government seat. But on the contrary, if Mr. Macdougall could not guarantee such rights, that the Delegates request him to remain where he is, or return 'till the right be guaranteed by Act of the Canadian Parliament.

The English Representatives refused to appoint Delegates to go to Pembina to consult with Mr. Macdougall, stating, they had no authority to do so from their constituents, upon which the Council was dissolved.

The meeting at which the above resolutions were adopted was held at Fort Garry, on Wednesday, Dec. 1, 1869.

Winnipeg, December 4th, 1869.

The Métis bill of rights

*Donald Smith, later Lord
Strathcona. What was his
greatest contribution to the
development of Canada?*

crowd that gathered to hear them. Smith convinced the
people that their fears were groundless; after his speech,
the crisis seemed to be over.

It was only a temporary lull. The Canadians in the
colony were still smarting over their treatment and that
accorded to Governor McDougall. Many of those who
had been taken prisoner had escaped and made their way
back to Portage la Prairie, where they made plans to
attack Fort Garry. On February 12, 1870, they marched
from the portage to Kildonan Presbyterian Church, a
short distance from the fort.

Three days later, as they waited for the right moment
to attack, the door was thrust roughly open and two of
the Canadians dragged in a young Métis, Norbert
Parisien. They had found him nearby and were convinced

he had been sent to spy on them. They kept him imprisoned under the pulpit overnight while they debated what to do with him. In the morning, they let him outside under guard; Parisien managed to seize a gun and dash away from his captors.

He headed blindly for the river. There he saw a Canadian, Hugh Sutherland, on the frozen ice. Convinced that Sutherland had been sent to catch him, he fired at the Canadian, then fled on. But the other Canadians caught up with him, dragged him back to the church and beat him badly. Within a few days, both Sutherland and Parisien had died of their wounds.

Rumours raced around the settlement. Some said that Parisien had been beaten with an axe; others that he had been shot in cold blood. No one was sure of the truth, but the two deaths frightened the Canadians and they decided to give up their plan of attacking the fort and go back home.

Their route led them close to the fort. As the horses trudged through the snow, pulling the loaded sleighs, a patrol of Métis rode out to intercept them. The Métis gestured the Canadians toward the fort. One of the Canadians raised his gun, but Boulton quickly signalled to him to put it down. The Canadians changed course and entered the fort. As soon as they passed through the gates, they were arrested and imprisoned.

Louis Riel was certain that the Canadians had come to attack the fort and he threatened to have Boulton shot. Donald Smith convinced Riel that this would be an unwise move, and Riel backed down. The next man to rouse Riel's anger would not be so lucky.

1870: Chapter 7
The Death of Thomas Scott

The Métis guard paced slowly past the rooms that housed
the Canadian prisoners. His rifle lay solidly across his
shoulders: these prisoners would not escape as they had
done before. But his thoughts were only half on the
prisoners. He was preoccupied with the ideas behind the
nation he was helping to build.

Suddenly a sound caught his attention. He looked up.
Above him one of the most troublesome of the prisoners,
Thomas Scott, was calmly spitting out of the window at
the guard's feet.

"Don't do that again!" The guard unslung his rifle.

Scott spat again. "And who is to stop me?"

"I tell you, do not do that!"

"I'll do what I like, you dirty half-breed Frenchman."

"What are you saying?"

"Learn to speak English. I'll do whatever I like, you
son of a prairie dog. Soon the soldiers will come from
Ontario and capture this fort. Then you and your friends
will swing in the breeze and I'll be there to laugh at your
hanging."

The guard understood only a few of the words Scott
hurled at him in English. But there was no mistaking the
tone. He let out a bellow of rage and rushed in through
the door and up the stairs to the room where Scott was
held. Half a dozen Métis followed him.

"Leave the fool alone." "I'll kill him!" "You filthy
half-breed!" The air was filled with shouts. Then all was
quiet. The guard halted, his hands almost on Scott's
throat. Louis Riel had entered the room. He waved the
guards outside. Alone with Scott, he studied the prisoner
intently.

"You always make trouble. Why? Your friends have

Thomas Scott

been reasonable men; they have agreed not to fight the new government and they have gone free. But you must shout and swear and call names and battle with the guards. You must keep trying to escape and threaten to kill us once you are free. You insult the guards and make them lose their heads. Why? We are the government here now and you have no choice but to obey. Can you not see that? You have no choice."

"You, the government? Don't make me laugh. You? A bunch of Catholic half-breeds? It would be a sunny day in hell before I'd do a thing you tell me to. What can you do to me you haven't done already? You and your bunch of cowards don't scare me one bit."

Riel stayed calm. "There is a crime among the Métis on the hunt; it is called insubordination. You are certainly guilty of that."

"This is not the hunt and I am not a Métis — thank God. When the soldiers come from Canada, you will learn what crimes are and you will be punished," Scott retorted.

Riel turned white. His hands clenched into fists, then dropped back to his sides." Do not push us too far, Mr. Scott. Your life is not worth much to me."

Scott laughed unpleasantly.

"We shall see who is master here, Mr. Scott. We shall see." Riel turned and walked from the room.

The next day, Riel convened a court-martial, charging Scott with the crime of insubordination, punishable by death. The jury considered the evidence of the witnesses: Scott consistently refused to do what he was told, fought with the guards and insulted them, tried to escape. There could be only one verdict. By the rules of the hunt, Scott was guilty of a most serious crime. The sentence was death in front of a firing squad.

The news of the verdict spread quickly. Smith tried to argue with Riel; others came and tried to persuade him to change his mind. But he stood firm. "This man has given us no choice. He has called us cowards. He and all Canadians must learn that the Métis are men of their words. Tomorrow Mr. Scott dies."

The next day, Scott was marched through the gates of the fort, a minister at his side. Only now did he realize that his bluff had been called, that Riel had not been making an idle threat. "They can't do this," he muttered as he walked. "They cannot do this."

He was wrong. A white bandage was placed over his eyes. The rifles were raised. The squad fired. One man stepped forward to deliver the coup de grace with his revolver. Thomas Scott lay dead, executed by order of the Provisional Government, president Louis Riel.

The execution of Thomas Scott. How do you think the artist who drew this picture felt about the death of Scott?

Aftermath Chapter 8

The death of Thomas Scott brought a hush to activities at Red River. Only a few days after the firing squad had carried out the sentence of death, Bishop Taché returned to Red River after a long journey in Europe and Canada. This time he came as a delegate from Ottawa, and he brought good news. He promised that there would be an amnesty for those who had formed the Provisional Government, that the Canadian government would take no action against them. He urged the Westerners to send delegates to Ottawa with their demands and suggested that the delegates would be well received. Three men — the Abbé Ritchot, Judge John Black, and Alfred Scott — set out for the East carrying the list of terms and conditions under which Red River was willing to join Canada.

The list was based on the bill of rights the settlers had drawn up the preceding fall. There were new and important additions. Riel and his followers now insisted that the area would join Canada only as a province, with the same rights and privileges as the other provinces. They also demanded that the province be permitted to have separate schools, so that each religious denomination might have its own schools.

Once the delegates left, things seemed to return to normal in the North-West. In the East, things were less calm. The news of the execution of Thomas Scott had reached Ontario and roused the people there. John Schultz was now in Canada, and he shouted in the newspapers and at meetings that Scott had been killed because he was a Protestant and a Canadian; that he had been killed by Catholics and Frenchmen. Newspaper editorials demanded that troops be sent to the North-West to quell these unruly Métis and restore law and order. There were calls for the execution of Riel. The government of Ontario offered $5,000 for his capture.

The Abbé Ritchot and Alfred Scott had scarcely reached Ottawa when they were arrested and charged with the murder of Thomas Scott. The charge was quickly dismissed, but it showed the mood of Protestant, English Ontario. Its people wanted revenge.

In Quebec, French Canadians were demanding that Riel and all his followers be given an amnesty. It was intolerable, they said, that the Métis should be punished just because they were French and Catholic.

Prime Minister Macdonald, sensing that whatever he did would anger some part of the population, tried to do nothing. He was forced to give in to one demand, however: that troops be sent to the North-West. A company under the command of Colonel Garnet Wolseley was dispatched, destination Red River.

Sir John A. Macdonald trying "to do nothing." Who is the man in the background?

A CASE OF RIEL DISTRESS!

On May 12, 1870, the Red River area became a full province of Canada, with an elected assembly, members of parliament in Ottawa, land grants for the Métis and many of the other concessions that the delegates to Ottawa had demanded. Riel and his followers had won the battle.

For Riel, it was a shaky victory. Although the Canadian government had agreed that the westerners should have much of what they had fought for, Riel was still in personal danger. No one was sure whether Wolseley's expedition was coming on a peaceful mission or on a mission of vengeance. There were rumours that many of the Canadian soldiers were intent on collecting the reward offered for capturing Riel.

The troops were a few kilometres away from Fort

Garnet Wolseley. In 1879, he wrote in his diary: "God grant at least that my name may not be handed down . . . in connection with a disgraceful disaster." How far was this hope fulfilled?

*The house in St. Vital where
Riel stayed*

Garry when a Hudson's Bay Company employee rushed
into Riel's house, breathless from a rapid ride. "For the
love of God, clear out," he gasped. "The troops are just
outside the city and you are going to be lynched." Furious
and bitter at the thought that he had been betrayed, Riel
fled, first to Bishop Taché's house and then on to St. Vital.

As he left the bishop's house, he could see the soldiers
entering Fort Garry. "No matter what happens now," he
said to the bishop, "the rights of the Métis are assured
by the Manitoba Act; that is what I wanted. My mission
is finished."

Colonel Wolseley was less statesmanlike. "Personally,
I was glad that Riel did not come out and surrender as he
at one time said he would," he wrote, "for I could not
have then hanged him as I might have done had I taken
him prisoner when in arms against his sovereign."

Election Chapter 9
and Exile

Riel did not want to leave his new province of Manitoba yet he knew that he must. Every minute that he stayed on Canadian soil his life was in danger. Reluctantly, he headed for the United States, spurred on by a letter from Taché that told him the amnesty for Riel and his followers had not been confirmed and that he was eagerly sought by many of the Canadians who wanted both his life and the glory of capturing the famed rebel.

"Time alone will help us; patience, then, God will not abandon us," Riel wrote back to Taché. "My life belongs to God. Let him do what he wishes with it."

Riel remained in the United States for a full year. Rumours reached him from Red River: one Métis had been stoned into the river where he drowned; others had been attacked by newcomers to the settlement. Weighed down by his own problems and his worries over his family and his friends, Riel fell ill and almost died. He was on his way to recovery when he heard that federal elections were being held at Red River to select the province's representatives in Ottawa.

Riel wanted badly to stand for parliament but decided against it when George Cartier was defeated in his own Quebec riding and came west to run in Red River. Cartier won the seat but soon after, he died. This time, Riel was determined to run for election. He returned to Red River, campaigning when he could and keeping out of sight when he thought it wise. He won easily.

In Riel's time, elections in different parts of the country were held on different days.

He could not go openly to claim his seat in parliament, for there was still a warrant for his arrest in Ontario and a $5,000 reward offered for his capture. Riel's friends smuggled him into Ontario but at the last minute Riel decided to return to Montreal to wait for a safer time to make his appearance. He went south to the United States for a time, to visit Father Barnabé, the priest in the village of Keeseville. Time passed slowly and boringly for Riel.

Election and Exile

Then a new election was called and Riel determined to run for office once more. Again he was elected and this time he was determined to show his face in Ottawa. It was winter; muffled in heavy clothes that helped to disguise him, he slipped into the Parliament Buildings and signed the roll. As he left, the Clerk of the House glanced down at the signature, then, astounded, looked up to see Riel gravely bowing to him at the door.

It was not as simple to take his seat in the House. Reports circulated that armed men waited in the gallery to apprehend — or kill — Riel should he attempt to enter

Louis Riel

parliament again. Several dark, bearded men were arrested because they looked rather like him. Riel decided to retreat to Montreal once more.

He was ordered to take his seat. Still he did not appear. Finally, he was thrown out of parliament and his seat declared vacant.

That same year, an amnesty for Riel was finally approved, on condition that he stayed out of Canada for five years.

Should he accept the amnesty? The events of the months since the Provisional Government had taken office had exhausted Riel. His enemies seemed to be everywhere and his friends powerless. As long as he stayed in Canada, he would keep the hate and desire for revenge alive and the wound inflicted by the shooting of Thomas Scott would never heal. Wearily and reluctantly, he decided to return to the United States to wait out his period of exile.

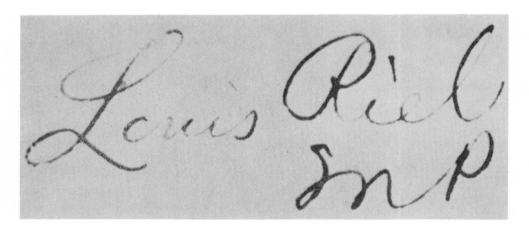

Chapter 10 **The Vision and the Madness**

Riel smoothed out the much folded paper in front of him. The moonlight that filtered through the window gave scarcely enough light to read. Over and over again he had read the letter, written by Bishop Bourget of Montreal. He carried it next to his heart every day, and its words were etched on his brain:

God will not abandon you in the darkest hours of your life. For he has given you a mission which you must fulfill in all respects.

And these, thought Riel, *are surely the darkest hours of my life. Far from my family, far from my friends, no way of making a living, no way of supporting my family, forbidden to return to my own country.* Even the letter written by Bishop Bourget, a man whom Riel respected more than almost any other in the church, sometimes failed to draw him out of the gloom that engulfed him.

But I will still believe, Riel said to himself. *God has given me a mission, to save the Métis from the Canadians who will overwhelm them. God has chosen me and he will guide me on the way. But O God, let it be soon; I cannot wait forever.* He refolded the letter and placed it under his pillow, then lay down for the night.

His was not an easy sleep. He tossed and turned, shouted out, tormented by his dreams of God and Christ, of his enemies, of the bleeding body of Thomas Scott, of his friends, of his dead father, of his beloved mother, of his dear sisters and brothers. He awoke spent, worn out.

His day was spent like all his days in exile, praying, searching for the truth through God. As he knelt in front of the altar that day, he was suddenly seized with intense joy. He covered his face with his handkerchief to hide the intensity of the emotion. The next moment, he was swept down into sorrow so deep that his wracking sobs sounded through the church.

"Oh, my God," he sobbed, "help me, help me to see the way."

But he saw no way. In his place of exile with Father Barnabé in Keeseville, he could not hide his growing pain. He woke at night crying, his pillow wet with tears. He shouted with the terror in his mind, unable to find his way through the darkness that seemed to be everywhere about him.

Father Barnabé sent for Riel's uncle John Lee, with whom he had stayed when he first left the seminary in Montreal. Dismayed by what he saw, John Lee decided to smuggle his nephew back to Montreal where he could be helped. But Riel could not stay quiet.

He ran through the corridors of the train, his uncle trailing vainly behind. "I am a prophet, I am a prophet," he bellowed as the train bustled north. Then he fell onto his seat and prayed aloud starting up suddenly to bellow and snort like a bull. John Lee explained timidly to the other passengers that this poor man was sick and prayed silently that no one would recognize Louis Riel in this demented being.

Somehow the pair reached Montreal unrecognized and went immediately to John Lee's home. There Riel seemed sometimes to be better. But much of the time he tore at his clothes and shouted and argued with the priests he sought out at church, trying to find a way out of the darkness that still suffocated him. At last, his uncle and friends took him to hospital and registered him under the name of Louis David. But a public hospital seemed too dangerous a place for a man under sentence of exile, and he was transferred to the asylum at Beauport, near Quebec City.

He still could not find his way out of his terror. Most of the time, he waited quietly in his room, writing letters full of prophecy about politics and religion. He called himself Louis David Riel, Prophet, Infallible Pontiff and Priest-King. He saw that the world was sinful, that Canada was God's chosen country and the French Canadians God's chosen people. He thought that every man's hand was against him, that he was all alone in the world.

Sometimes, he could not stand the pain of silence any longer and he would tear off his clothes to run naked through the corridors, to smash the ornaments on the altar in the chapel, to struggle with the guards. Somehow, somehow, he must find a way out from the walls of loneliness and fear that enclosed him.

He hated the asylum and yet it seemed to help him. The visions and the fits grew less frequent. The walls seemed to recede a little, to let the light in. He was allowed to go out occasionally to visit friends; he looked about him with a new sense of wonder, at the trees, the ground, the faces of people. In some way that he did not understand, the darkness had cleared and he was free again.

He was allowed to leave the hospital, but warned that he must lead a quiet life, perhaps as a farmer. "I thank God for having humiliated me and for having brought me to understand what human glory is," he wrote to Bishop Taché, telling him he had decided to move to the Western United States. "How quickly it passes; and how vain it is for him who having for a little while captured the attention of men, suddenly feels the hand of God weighing upon him."

Riel went to stay again with Father Barnabé. There, he grew to love the priest's sister, Evelina, and to talk with her about marriage. But Riel still felt the pull of the West and he set off once more. He wrote to Evelina for a time, but in his heart he knew that this gentle, quiet girl from the civilized East could not live in the type of home Riel would find on the western prairie. He stopped writing and turned his attention to the Métis of the American West.

Louis Riel about 1878

Chapter 11 1884:
Going Home

It was a warm June day and the small church at St. Peter's Mission, Montana, was stuffy. The Métis and Indian parishioners crowded into the pews followed the words of the Mass. It was only halfway through when a Métis from the settlement slipped into the pew beside Louis Riel.

"Can you come outside?" he asked. "There are people here to see you."

"Can't they wait until the service is over?"

Riel's friend shrugged. "They have come a long way, from north of the border, I think."

Riel rose immediately and followed the man. He got so little news from home. His exile had ended five years

ST. PETER'S MISSION, MONTANA

ago but even so Riel had been home only once the previous summer. Then it seemed that most of his friends had moved away from Red River. Perhaps the visitors would have news either of these friends or of Riel's family.

The little group of newcomers had taken refuge from the sun in the shade of a small grove of trees. One of them moved toward Riel. "Louis, you remember me?"

Riel frowned searching through his memory for the name that went with this face from the past. Then he recognized Gabriel Dumont, one of the Métis who had been with him at Red River.

"Of course, Gabriel. What brings you here?"

Dumont motioned Riel back into the shade. "You know that things have changed since you left Red River. Most of us left soon after you. There were too many people coming in to settle, too many farmers, too many Canadians. The government gave us all grants of land, but many of us had no liking for that settled sort of life. We moved further north and west, to the banks of the Saskatchewan River, where we would live as we have always lived and not be bothered by anyone."

The other men nodded. One grunted, "Nobody to tell us what to do. Still a chance to hunt the buffalo."

Louis Riel, about 1884

"But now Red River is happening all over again," continued Dumont. "Only this time it is worse. They are building a railway across the land, so no one will need our carts anymore. Settlers are moving in and the government pretends not to know we are there. Worse, the buffalo have gone. No one knows where. The Indians are starving and we will be next. Even the white people are unhappy with the government. The crops are bad and everyone is poor."

Dumont took a deep breath. "Louis Riel, we need you. Come back and help us. You are the only person who can lead all the Métis, the only one who can talk to the white settlers and persuade them we should all join together to fight the government. Come back with us."

Riel scowled. "This is my home now. I am a school-teacher here. I have become an American citizen. I am married and I have children."

Dumont waved a hand at the horizon. "The United States, Canada, what does a border mean to a Métis? The only thing that matters is that we, your brothers, need

you and have come to ask you to lead us once more."

Riel felt the old familiar excitement rising in him. Sternly, he tried to beat it back. "I must think. I will let you know tomorrow."

He turned away from the group, but he did not go back toward the church and the settlement. Instead, he walked out onto the prairie. He needed time to think, time to consider.

As he walked, his mind travelled back over the years since he had left Red River. The years of his enforced exile and his illness he preferred not to think about. He had promised then that he would lead a quiet life, with nothing to upset him. He had not quite kept that promise, but over the last seven years he had built a life for himself in the United States.

Marguerite Monet Riel

For three years, he had roamed the plains with the Métis, hunting and packing. Then he had married Marguerite Monet, a young Métis girl; they had two children.

He had decided to take out American citizenship and fight for the rights of the American Métis. He had aroused strong feelings, with one newspaper and one political party calling him a hero and the other newspaper and the other political party demanding he be thrown in jail.

He had accepted the post of schoolteacher at the mission of St. Peter on the Sun River. From dawn to dark, he was responsible for the young Métis and Indians he taught. He found the children and the job tiring, but he prayed that he was accomplishing something worthwhile.

The years somersaulted through Riel's mind as he scuffed at the dust of the prairie and stared at the vast expanse before him with unseeing eyes. Now this summons came out of the past, and suddenly all was clear to him. He had just been marking time, waiting for his people to call upon him once more. He was not meant for the life of a schoolteacher. So many times so long ago, he had promised to God and himself that he would fufill God's mission. The time had come to keep that promise. He would go to the Saskatchewan.

Gabriel Dumont

Chapter 12 1884-85: On the Saskatchewan

Charles Nolin

The Riels arrived at Batoche on the Saskatchewan in the beginning of July, 1884; they stayed with Riel's cousin, Charles Nolin. Métis and white settlers alike soon heard of his arrival and came to talk about their problems. This time, Riel did not have to convince the different groups that they should join together. Meetings in the months before among the Métis, both French and English, and the other settlers had already convinced them of this.

They had different complaints. The Métis wanted recognition of their right to land along the Saskatchewan and acceptance of the French language. They also wanted to be represented on any council that would govern the North-West.

The settlers who had come west to take up land along the Saskatchewan were disappointed with the results. Although the crops had been good in the ten years up to 1881, a series of disasters in the last few years had impoverished the farmers. The railway had gone through far to the south, and no new money was coming to the Saskatchewan from this source. There was not even an easy way of transporting to market whatever crops the farmers were able to raise.

What angered them most was the fact that the government in Ottawa did not seem to care at all about their problems. Petitions, requests, telegrams, letters, official suggestions from government representatives in the North-West, pleas from the priests and bishops in the area: all were ignored. There seemed to be no way to wake up Ottawa.

No way, that is, except rebellion. Already the newspapers of the North-West were beginning to say that perhaps the sound of a few gunshots would catch

Ottawa's attention. And perhaps the name of Louis Riel would burn a few ears and make a few people sit up straight.

The Indians of the North-West were just as unhappy. Like the Métis, the Indians had relied on the buffalo for food. Once the railway spread west, buffalo had been killed in huge numbers and the great herds destroyed. Now the hunters came home empty-handed.

The Canadian government declared that the Indians should live from farming instead. Many of the Indian bands had signed treaties with the government, giving up their rights to the land in return for reservations and promises of food and help.

But a people who have lived all their lives as hunters do not find it easy to become farmers overnight. By 1883, many of the Indians were starving. The North West Mounted Police handed out some rations — "I can hand out only two days' rations each seven days," wrote one superintendent — but it was not enough to do much good.

In anger, some of the Indians began to talk about an uprising against the Canadian government. The Cree Chief Big Bear had been one of the last to sign a treaty with the government, and now he steadfastly refused to withdraw to the reserve assigned to him and his tribe. Instead, as other discontented Indians gathered around him, he began to talk about a great Indian confederacy.

A council was held in June, on the reserve of Pound-maker, a Blackfoot chief, and the Indians began to discuss the concessions they wanted from the government. The council broke up when the Mounted Police arrived, but rumour had it that it would reassemble elsewhere. And perhaps next time Crowfoot, one of the leading and most respected Cree chiefs, who had become very bitter about the treatment the Indians were receiving from the government, might join with Poundmaker and Big Bear.

All these ingredients awaited Riel when he arrived in Batoche. Over the next few weeks, he spoke calmly and with moderation to all the groups along the Saskatchewan. He was cheered wherever he went, as people rallied to his leadership.

Riel himself was particularly pleased. "Not long ago, I was a humble schoolmaster on the faraway banks of the Missouri," he wrote to his brother and brother-in-law in

Above: Chief Big Bear
Right: Chief Poundmaker

Manitoba. "Here I am today in the ranks of the most popular public men in the Saskatchewan. What has brought all this about? You know that it is God. I humble myself to the ground. The Lord has done great things for me. What shall I render to God for the favours he has heaped on me?"

Riel and his followers tried once more to convince Ottawa that the needs of the West must be met. They drew up a petition which was sent to Ottawa, asking for better treatment of the Indians, land grants for the Métis and representation in the government of the North-West.

There was no reply. Vague promises drifted back to the North-West, but it seemed clear that Ottawa had no intention of taking any definite action.

By March of 1885, the people of the Saskatchewan were tired of waiting. Perhaps it was time, Riel said in a speech, "to bare our teeth." Now even the church seemed to have turned against the settlers and the Métis. One priest, Father Fourmond, said in church that any Catholic who took part in an armed uprising could no longer consider himself a Catholic. Riel was suddenly furiously angry. He charged that Fourmond had brought lies and politics into the church.

Riel decided that he must speak to God himself and no longer go through the church. The church would not support Riel; so be it. Riel would not support the church. He became more and more religious, speaking constantly of God and praying to him, but he would not enter a church. To some, he seemed a saint, more godly than any priest.

Events began to move more swiftly as Riel's anger and his belief that God was directing him led him on. On March 18, 1885, he and his followers took several government officials prisoner, commandeered a church and cut the telegraph lines to Prince Albert.

A band of armed men gathered at Batoche to form a provisional government. Charles Nolin tried to oppose the new government and was arrested.

On March 20, Riel sent a message to Superintendent Lief Crozier of the North West Mounted Police, demanding that Crozier surrender Fort Carlton. If Crozier refused, Riel told him, the Métis would attack the fort and begin "a war of extermination upon all those who have shown themselves hostile to our rights."

Crozier refused the demand.

Chapter 13 **The North-West Rebellion**

The rider was small in the distance, but even from a long way off it was clear that he was in a hurry. Before his horse slowed to a stop inside Fort Carlton, he had flung himself off and dashed into the room where Superintendent Crozier was sitting.

"The Métis have attacked us," he shouted. "They've cut us off, they've got us pinned down —"

Crozier started up from his chair. Earlier that day, he had sent men with sleighs to get provisions from a store at Duck Lake. They must have met with trouble.

"Where are they, man?" he demanded. "What's happened?"

"That crazy man Dumont and his breeds stopped us on the way to Duck Lake and Dumont fired at us. Everyone stopped in his tracks, but I managed to get away and gallop for the fort."

Crozier strode out of the room. "Lieutenant, Sergeant,

THE NORTH-WEST
REBELLION

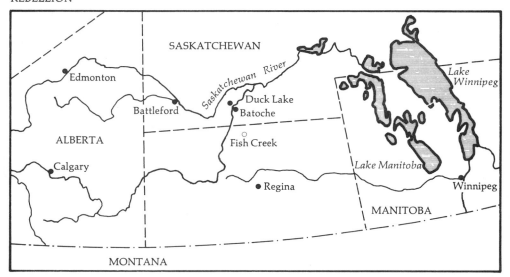

muster up all the men and call for volunteers from the town. Hitch up the cannon. We'll be on the trail in half an hour."

Exactly half an hour later, the police and the volunteers from nearby Prince Albert were on their way. At Duck Lake, Riel and 300 Métis had joined Dumont and his force of 30. Dumont had long ago let the Mounted Police sleighs return to Fort Carlton, and Dumont and Riel were talking quietly when news arrived that the police were coming.

Two Métis went out with a white blanket held high. Due to a misunderstanding, a shot was fired. Crozier saw the Métis approaching from all sides.

"Fire!" he shouted and the battle was on.

From the beginning, the battle went well for Riel and Dumont's men. The police and volunteers were trapped in a hollow; the Métis surrounded them and poured down their fire from above. Methodically, each man fired from a prone position, reloaded, ran to a better position, dropped to the ground and fired again.

The Battle of Duck Lake

Had the fighters looked up through the smoke, they would have seen a strange sight. Louis Riel, mounted on horseback, a cross held high in his hands, advanced slowly toward the enemy. He had no gun, no weapon at all. Yet the bullets did not touch him. He was sure that his prayers would protect him, that his cause was just and that God would not strike him down.

Crozier soon recognized defeat. He ordered a retreat, leaving twelve dead behind him. Five Métis were killed.

The victory at Duck Lake convinced Riel that victory in the war would be his. "The police have attacked us," he wrote to one group of Métis. "God gave us the victory. . . . Rise; face the enemy, and if you can do so, take Battleford, destroy it."

"Take all the ammunition you can, whatever store-houses it be in," he wrote to others. "Murmur, growl and threaten. Stir up the Indians. Render the police of Fort Pitt and Battleford harmless."

Duck Lake brought others into the battle. Big Bear and Poundmaker decided to throw in their lot with Riel, against the government and the police who had disrupted their lives and left them starving. They would rather die in battle than live as beggars.

Duck Lake was the beginning of a new dream for Louis Riel. It was also the end. Fifteen years earlier, the show of rebellion had won him victory, as the Canadian government gave in to the demands of the Métis and the settlers. But this time, open warfare was involved; men were being killed. And this time, circumstances had changed.

Fifteen years before, the North-West had been isolated, attainable only by a long and difficult journey from the east. Now the railway stretched its shining steel from east to west, and news and armies travelled quickly.

And this time, the name of Riel stirred memories. As the eyes of the East turned upon the North-West, the westerners were doomed. There was no excuse for armed rebellion, whatever the cause, said the easterners. Those who rebelled must be defeated.

Eight thousand men rushed forward to join the forces that would fight Riel. They were hurried west, then north to the Saskatchewan. One part of the force was dispatched

Canadian troops under General Middleton moving towards Winnipeg

to Battleford, now surrounded by Indians. The other sped toward Batoche, Riel's headquarters.

Scouts brought daily reports of the troops' approach to Batoche. Dumont, now Riel's lieutenant and in charge of the Métis army, wanted to move at once. He was a man experienced in plains warfare; he knew the value of avoiding an eye-to-eye battle with a larger and better-armed force.

"We must harass them, make them uneasy, make them lose heart," he told Riel. "They are not used to the West and they will give way easily. Do not give them time to sleep, make them worry, upset them."

Riel would not hear of it. "I have prayed to God," he told Dumont, "and I have been told that I must wait until the soldiers attack us. Then, with God's help, we will win."

Dumont eyed Riel unhappily. There were times, he thought, when a man should listen to God and times when he should listen to common sense. Surely this was a time to be reasonable. But even as he looked at Riel where he sat praying once more, he knew he could not

The Battle of Batoche

The Battle of Fish Creek

change Riel's mind. And this man was the leader of the Métis; Dumont would obey.

At last, Dumont led 150 of his men out to spy on the troops under the command of General Middleton. He found the army and decided to trap it in a coulee, as the Métis had so often trapped the buffalo.

This prey fought back. Many of Dumont's men fled from the unequal battle, and the Métis were forced to retreat. It was not a total defeat: five Métis were killed, but the Métis killed fifty soldiers.

At Batoche, Riel could hear the sound of the guns firing and the cannon booming. All day long he stood praying, his arms held high so that his body formed a cross. When he tired and his arms threatened to drop, his friends came forward to hold his arms up for him.

The prayers did little good. The Battle of Fish Creek showed clearly that, while the Métis had more skill in battle, Middleton had many more soldiers, weapons and ammunition. Defeat was only a matter of time.

The final assault on Batoche

The end came with the Battle of Batoche. For three days the Métis held off the approaching troops, using nails as ammunition in their desperation. Then, even the nails gone, they fled into the woods.

Dumont recognized defeat and decided to make his way to the United States. He urged Riel to go with him. But Riel was tired of running away. "I will go to fulfill God's will," he wrote to Middleton. On May 13, he surrendered to three Mounted Police scouts.

The Indians had no better success in battle. Soon after the defeat at Batoche, Poundmaker was forced to surrender at Battleford and Big Bear was taken prisoner. The rebellion was over.

The North-West Field Force under the command of General Middleton. Super-intendent Leif Crozier is in the back row (marked by a dot).

1885: Chapter 14
The Trial

The battle on the plains was over; the battle in the courts was just beginning. Louis Riel was charged with treason and taken to Regina, where he was kept in jail for eight weeks. He wrote to his family and friends and to politicians; he filled his notebooks with his dreams and his visions.

Outside, the Riel controversy raged again. In Quebec, a Riel Defence Committee was set up and three lawyers chosen to defend Riel. They decided there could be only one defence to the charge of treason, since it seemed obvious to them that Riel had indeed committed treason. He must have been insane; his visions, his belief that he was talking directly to God, his strange political ideas, his history of illness and breakdown, all proved he had not been in his right mind when he led the Métis into rebellion.

Riel after he had been taken prisoner

There was only one difficulty. Riel would not agree to this defence. Even as his trial started, he tried to interrupt his lawyers. "I cannot abandon my dignity," he pleaded with the judge. "Here I have to defend myself against the accusation of high treason or I have to consent to the animal life of an asylum."

Riel was forbidden to interrupt and the case began in a room packed with spectators. Witnesses testified to Riel's actions during the rebellion, to the notes he had written and the fiery speeches he had made. Priests testified that Riel was not a religious man at all, that he had defied the church. Charles Nolin, Riel's cousin and once his friend, testified against him. Three doctors took the stand to discuss Riel's sanity: one said he was of unsound mind, while the other two said there was nothing wrong with him.

At last it was Riel's turn to speak. He rose slowly in the witness box. For an hour, speaking in English, he prayed, pleaded, tried to explain what he had done.

"The North-West is my mother, it is my mother country. When I first came to the North-West, I found the Indians suffering. I found the half-breeds eating the rotten pork of the Hudson's Bay Company and getting sick and weak every day. I remembered that half-breed meant white and Indian and I have directed my attention to help the Indians, to help the half-breeds, to help the whites to the best of my ability."

Then Riel came to what he believed lay at the centre of his actions. "I believe I have a mission. I have yet and still have that mission and with the help of God who is in this box with me, and he is on the side of the lawyers to help me, I will fulfill this mission."

On and on he talked, about his life and his mission, about the battles and the bullets that flew "as thick as mosquitoes in the hot days of summer."

And he swore again and again that he was not insane. "Even if I were going to be sentenced by you, gentlemen of the jury, I have this satisfaction if I die — that if I will die, I will not be looked on by all men as insane, as a lunatic."

Riel succeeded only in boring the crowd. Heads nodded and men looked uneasily around for a way of escape. Rebellion and bullets and death in battle were exciting, but this talk of God and injustice and insanity was dull. Even the judge was scarcely polite as he asked Riel if he was through.

"Not yet. I worked to better the conditions of the Saskatchewan at the risk of my life, to better the condition of the people of the North-West. It will be for you to pronounce whether you believe what I have done is just."

At last Riel sat down. The trial dragged to a close. The judge made his charge to the jury, not a French Canadian nor Métis among them. The jury filed from their box into a back room to make their decision. As they left, Riel's voice sounded over the voices of the crowd and the buzzing of the flies as he knelt in the prisoner's box and prayed. He was still praying an hour later when the jury returned.

"Gentlemen, are you agreed upon your verdict? How say you, is the prisoner guilty or not guilty?"

"The jury find the prisoner guilty."

The scene in the courtroom at Riel's trial

"You find the prisoner Louis Riel guilty? So say you all?"

"Guilty."

"Louis Riel, have you anything to say why the sentence of the court should not be pronounced upon you for the offence of which you have been found guilty?"

Riel stood once more. This was his last chance. Surely he could make people understand that he had acted only to help his people. Surely they would see that he had been right.

"I suppose that, having been condemned as a traitor, I will cease to be called a fool," he began slowly. He had gained one victory: he was not crazy. Now he would try to convince the people of the rest.

He spoke of everything that had ever happened to him, every event in the North-West, his hopes, his dreams, his prayers, his mission, his God, his plans for the country.

No one was listening. Riel was guilty and the excitement was over. Riel looked about him and came to a stumbling halt. No one cared. He sat down.

The judge spoke again. "You have been found guilty of high treason. You have been proved to have let loose the floodgates of rapine and bloodshed. For what you did, what you have said is no excuse whatever.

"It is now my painful duty to pass the sentence of the court upon you. That is, you be taken from here to the police guardrooms at Regina, that you be kept there till the 18th of September next, that on the 18th of September next, you be taken to the place appointed for your execution and there be hanged by the neck until you are dead. And may God have mercy on your soul."

Riel wrote to his brother Joseph asking him to look after Marguerite and the children, Jean and Angelique. Joseph Riel took them to his home. What became of Louis Riel's wife and children?

The Execution of Louis Riel

Twice the execution of Louis Riel was postponed as the arguments raged. Some continued to insist that Riel was insane and must not be hanged. Others claimed that Riel was to die simply because he was a Frenchman and a Catholic; that an English Protestant would never be executed. Some said that Riel had been right and should be rewarded and not punished. Still others said that the sooner he was hanged, the better off the whole country would be.

The debate dragged on, in the newspapers, in the House of Commons, in the streets. It meant little to Louis Riel. The argument was beyond him now, of no importance. He spent day after day in his cell writing, to his mother, to his wife, to the president of the United States, to the American consul in Winnipeg. But most of all, he wrote in his notebook about the visions that still consumed him.

He wanted above all to set the record straight. He predicted the future: Spain would come to help the North-West; Manitoba would become French-Canadian; in 500 years there would be 40 million Métis.

Even as he wrote, time was running out. The last appeal was lodged and refused; the last stay of execution granted. The execution was now set for November 15. Early that morning, he wrote his last letter, to his mother. "It is two hours past midnight. Good Father André told me this morning to hold myself ready for tomorrow. I listen to him. I obey. The Lord is helping me to maintain a peaceful and a calm spirit, like the oil in a vase which cannot be agitated."

Louis Riel, drawn from life, 1885

la souffrance.

Je vous embrasse tous avec la plus grande affection.

Vous chère maman, je vous embrasse comme doit faire un fils dont l'âme est pleine d'amour filial.

Vous ma chère épouse, je vous embrasse comme doit le faire un époux chrétien, selon l'esprit catholique de l'union conjugale.

Mes chers petits enfants, je vous embrasse comme doit le faire un père chrétien, en vous bénissant selon l'étendue de la miséricorde divine, pour la vie présente et pour la vie future.

Vous, mes chers frères, et sœurs, beaux frères et belles sœurs, neveux et nièces, parents, proches et amis, je vous embrasse avec tous les bons sentiments dont mon cœur est capable.

Soyez tous heureux. — chère maman,

Je suis votre fils affectueux soumis et obéissant   Louis "David" Riel.

The last page of the last letter Riel wrote to his mother from Regina jail

At eight o'clock, the cell door opened. Slowly Riel, the deputy sheriff, the chaplain, a policeman and Father André walked up the stairs toward the scaffold.

"Do you willingly sacrifice your life?" asked Father André.

"With all my heart, Father. I thank God for having given me the strength to die well. I die at peace with God and man."

The hangman tied Riel's hands, masked him and placed the noose over his head.

As Father André recited the Lord's Prayer, Louis Riel, saint, sinner, rebel, hero, prophet, madman, visionary, traitor, dropped to his death.

Riel's mother had earlier written to him: "I weep; yes, it is true, yet I lift my head high. . . . Courage once again, my dear son, courage, courage, in the great glory of God".

Further Reading

Barnett, D. *Poundmaker*. Toronto. Fitzhenry & Whiteside, 1976.

Bowsfield, H. *Louis Riel*. Toronto. Oxford University Press, 1971.

Dickie, D. *The Great Golden Plain/A History of the Prairie Provinces*. Toronto: Gage, 1962.

Knight, L. and Barnett, D. *A People and a Province*. Toronto: Fitzhenry & Whiteside, 1974.

McCourt, E. *Revolt in the West/The Story of the Riel Rebellion*. Toronto: Macmillan, 1958.

Morton, D. *The Queen v. Louis Riel*. Toronto: The University of Toronto Press, 1974.

Neering, R. *North West Mounted Police*. Toronto. Fitzhenry & Whiteside, 1974.

Neering, R. *Settlement of the West*. Toronto: Fitzhenry & Whiteside, 1974.

Stanley, G. F. G. *Louis Riel*. Toronto. McGraw-Hill Ryerson, 1972.

Waite, P. *John A. Macdonald*. Toronto: Fitzhenry & Whiteside, 1976.

Credits

The publishers wish to express their gratitude to the following who have given permission to use copyrighted illustrations in this book.

Glenbow-Alberta Institute, 59

Manitoba Archives, 9, 17, 20, 24, 28, 40, 41, 54 (bottom), 62

Metropolitan Toronto Library Board, 5, 7, 10, 11 (top), 19 (top), 25, 30, 34, 44, 56

Public Archives of Canada, title page (C 2048), 3, 11 (C 29698), 12 (C 1517), 23 (C 10144), 36, 37 (C 2048), 45 (C 15468), 46 (C 1704), 48, 51, 53, 54 (top), 55, 57, 61 (C 18085)

Royal Ontario Museum, 4

Saskatchewan Archives, 43

Editing: Laura Damania
Design: Jack Steiner
Cover Illustration: Robert Berger

The Canadians

Consulting Editor: Roderick Stewart
Editor-in-Chief: Robert Read

Every effort has been made to credit all sources correctly. The author and publishers will welcome any information that will allow them to correct any errors or omissions.